The Game of Credit

Corey P Smith

Editor: Corey P Smith

www.coreypsmith.com

Cover Design: Felix Walker

Book Design: Essex Graphix

Library of Congress Catalog Card Number: On File

Library of Congress Control Number: On File

Printed in the United States of America

The Credo Company LLC

3238 Players Club Circle

Memphis, TN 38125

www.coreypsmith.com

ISBN | 9798879952933

DISCLAIMER

This publication is designed to provide accurate and authoritative information with regard to the subject matter covered. While all of the stories described in the book are based on true experiences, most of the names are pseudonyms, and some situations have been changed slightly for educational purposes and to protect each individual's privacy. It is sold with the understanding that the publisher is not engaged in rendering legal or other professional advice. If legal advice or other expert assistance is required, the services of a competent professional person should be sought.

Contents

AUTHOR STATEMENT 1

CHAPTER I: DO NOT PASS GO, DO NOT COLLECT TWO HUNDRED DOLLARS 5

CHAPTER II: UNDERSTANDING THE GAME 11

CHAPTER III: HOW TO WRITE AN AFFIDAVIT 15

CHAPTER IV: HOW TO PREPARE A SWORN STATEMENT 21

CHAPTER V: HOW TO BEAT A COLLECTION AGENCY IN COURT 27

CHAPTER VI: SHOULD YOU USE DISCOVERY? 35

CHAPTER VII: FILING A MOTION TO STRIKE AFFIDAVIT OF DEBT 49

CHAPTER VIII: DISPUTE LETTERS 65

CHAPTER IX: ALWAYS BE THREE MOVES AHEAD.. 93

Author Statement

My father once told me that, “most people believe that being broke is the struggle, but the real struggle is having a problem that money can’t fix.” It took me a minute to understand exactly what he was saying to me at the time. I always figured life was going to be hard, if I didn’t have any money and I was taught in church that the bible said, “money answerth all things.” And yes, money does make life a whole lot easier, but life is not just about money, and it takes most of us our entire life to figure that part out. Life in fact is a game, but there are other parts of the game that we must understand, and it goes back to what I learned in church as a boy. And what I learned was spiritual laws and the bible provide all the rules to the game of life.

Think about it, the bible taught us that whatever we soweth we reap, if we give than we will receive, if we hate on another human being than we wil be hated on. And most of all “Keep the heart will all diligence, for out of it are the issues of life.” What does this mean? It means that whatever you dream or imagine, you can bring it into fruition.

When I was young there was a man who attended Tennessee State University with me, and he was always fearful of dying in a car accident. He was fearful because his cousin died in a fatal car accident. You see, he focused and pictured this in his mind so much that he drew this fatality into his life which led to his demise. So, as you work to improve your life and your name by tackling your credit issues, remember that you must train your mind to think positively and never allow your emotions to control your thoughts or actions. STAY POSITIVE!

"The Game of Life Is The Game Of Everlasting Learning. At Least It Is If You Want To Win"

Charlie Munger

Chapter One

Do Not Pass Go, Do Not Collect Two Hundred Dollars

There are two games in life that my father made sure I knew how to play. Those two games were Monopoly and the other one Chess. You see monopoly is fun, but after a few hours you can get content and bored at the same time. Now do not get confused, the only way that you can win the game is by eventually owning everything, that means the businesses, house, hotels and most of all the money.

The game can take you through a lot of emotions because it may sometimes seem unfair and disproportionate, due to the fact things just doesn't seem to go right at times. This sounds a lot like real life. Think about it, during the game one person seems to be getting richer and the other players are getting poorer. Some players are rolling the dice exactly right, while others are rolling the dice and going straight to jail or landing on someone else's property. Rolling the dice in the game is equivalent to us rolling the dice in life, but in real life it is called taking risk. You see just like in the game of monopoly; in life you have unlimited potential for growth. In the game that paper money is just like credit in life, you just have to figure out how to leverage it.

Life is just like the monopoly game that we think is real and guess what? It is real life. We as human beings are very complex people who like to compete and create different things like governments, cultures, countries, rules and regulations for all of them. Just like monopoly has rules, life has rules, but what gives you the power to enjoy the game is acquiring the most property and the most money. It's called ownership, and with ownership comes division. The division is the have and the have nots. Some of us have the freedom to do what we want, while others are controlled by a forty-hour work week.

You see, I told you that the play money in monopoly represents credit because it's not real and you can find yourself playing monopoly for hours without being able to gain full control of the board. This is just like life because humans invented the illusion or should I say, the idea of time and money.

One of the most powerful moves in monopoly is realizing that it is just a game. Just like in life the game of credit is made up, but it is up to you to figure out how to play it. Think about this, when the dice are thrown in a monopoly game the only player that the game gets tougher for is the weakest player, or the poorest player. The same is true in life every time you take a risk, but as soon as you figure out that it is all a game you can win. Just like the people who created the game of monopoly, a system was created by people that are no smarter than you in real life.

Remember life is real, but no one is stuck with unlucky dice. Everyone is free to learn, explore, create and most of all PASS GO!

"Most People Consider Life A Battle, But

It Is Not A Battle, It Is A Game"

Florence Scovel Shinn

Chapter Two

Understanding The Game

There is a way to tackle credit issues that does not involve dispute letters, Metro2 or E-Oscar. It is called litigation or what is known as Consumer Law. Some people can be intimidated by the entire practice of consumer law, but it is one of the most powerful legal actions that you can use to defeat creditors. When it comes to enforcing your rights as a consumer you want to find as many violations as possible against a creditor in connection with a debt, they say you owe.

The key to being successful is gathering as much evidence as you can to support your claims. This includes collecting documentation, such as billing statements, credit reports and any other correspondence between you and the creditor. I am going to break down exactly how you can use consumer law to your advantage, but I want you to understand a few things about litigation. I have spelled out a few things when it comes to consumer law such as terms and understanding affidavits as well as how to write one.

1. What is a Plaintiff? A plaintiff is the party who files the lawsuit.
2. What is a Defendant? A defendant is the party who is being sued by the plaintiff.
3. What is a Summons? A Summons is your official notification that you have been sued.
4. What is a Complaint? A Complaint explains why you have been sued. It contains the facts and the legal claims that are the basis for the lawsuit.

5. What is an Answer? An Answer is an official written response to a Complaint.
6. What is a Cross-Complaint? A Cross-Complaint is a claim that you have against the plaintiff.
7. What should I do if I receive a Summons and Complaint? DO NOT IGNORE IT. You should always respond to a Summons and Complaint.
8. Is there a time limit for filing an Answer? Yes. If you were served with the Summons and Complaint in person, you must file your Answer within 30 DAYS.
9. What if the time for filing my Answer has already expired? You should try to file an Answer anyway.

"In The Game Of Life, The Only

Way To Lose Is To Give Up"

UnKnown

Chapter Three

How To Write An Affidavit

An affidavit is a statement made under oath, claiming that a fact, or set of facts is true to the best of the "affiant's" knowledge. This sworn statement of facts is provided to the Courts or other government agencies to aid in proceedings like divorces, custody battles, and division of estate matters. Affidavits are usually sworn to before a Notary Public or before another officer that has authority to administer oath.

If false testimony was given in an affidavit form, the affiant, or the person who executed it, exposes himself to prosecution for the crime of perjury or giving a false statement under oath.

Keep in mind, there are situation-specific affidavits that may best serve your purpose for writing one, which is outlined at the end. However, to write a non-specific affidavit that can be used to serve nearly any purpose follow the steps below.

1. If the affidavit is a sworn statement, then the name and address of the person giving the testimony must be included in the title, e.g. Affidavit of Corey Smith.
2. If the affidavit will be submitted before the court, the caption of the case must be stated at the top. The case caption may be found on any of the pleadings filed by the parties in said case. The caption must include the name of the court, the county and the state, the names of the parties, and the case number.

3. In the first paragraph of the affidavit, include personal information about the affiant: his address, place of work, date of birth, occupation, immigration status, and the relationship of the affiant to any of the parties in the case.
4. Write an opening sentence, which must be in the first person. Then, state that the affiant is swearing under oath or affirming the information in the affidavit.
5. Make an outline of the facts to be stated in the affidavit. Determine which among the listed facts, are relevant and important, and disregard those that are not. Arrange the facts in a coherent manner.
6. State each fact in its own paragraph. Number the paragraphs so that it will be easier to read it and to refer to it in court.

7. Describe each fact concisely by providing names, dates, addresses, and other information as needed.
8. Reference supporting documents by marking them as "exhibits."
9. Next, make a statement that the affidavit is a complete representation of the facts to which the affiant is swearing. Also, spell out the oath that the affiant is taking.

At the end create the signature block. This is the space where the affiant signs his name and the last for you to do is provide a notary signature block.

"You Have To Learn The Rules Of The Game. And Then You Have To Play Better Than Anyone Else"

Albert Einstien

Chapter Four

HOW TO PREPARE A SWORN STATEMENT

A sworn statement or declaration is being allowed in more circumstances due to overloaded, expensive and time- consuming court proceedings. The sworn statement is similar to an affidavit, but not exactly the same. Here is how to prepare a sworn statement.

"Statement Under Penalty of Perjury"

Usually, judges prefer to have a witness testify in a formal court setting. In the court room, the witnesses will testify under oath meaning that if they lie, they could be found guilty of the crime of perjury. The court reporter will also make an official public record of the testimony.

Cross-examination is one of the other primary advantages where the judge, prosecuting attorney and defendant attorney have ample time to cross-examine the witness. All can physically listen to verbal and see non-verbal gestures, which give hints on the veracity of the testimony. The witness can testify to the facts and have this testimony juxtaposed to the testimony of other witnesses.

Sometimes, uncontrollable circumstances prevent individuals from being able to appear in court. These could include age, illness, incarceration or scheduling conflicts. The inconveniences of the long drawn out, expensive court case process has also helped open the door for more cost-effective sworn statements for preliminary hearings. Time is also a factor, memories deteriorate. A sworn statement would allow court proceedings to continue without the physical presence of a witness. Firsthand accounts are most valuable when the information is still fresh in the mind of the individual.

The author of a sworn statement testifies to the facts of an event, action or lawsuit. The author is called the "declarant." He makes his statement using the most descriptive and accurate language possible. At the end of the sworn written declaration, the declarant will write a separate endorsement paragraph using a phrase like the following: "I declare under penalty of perjury that the aforementioned is true." This sworn document will be filed with the clerk of the court.

An affidavit is the more traditional legal document for testimony. The affidavit would require a notary public or court clerk to witness, sign, stamp and seal the document. The individual giving an affidavit is called the "affiant." The public official can check the affiant's identity and determine if he is of sound mind. You should always check to see if your jurisdiction allows for sworn statements in lieu of affidavits.

If you are wondering why I took you on a verbal tour of the court room and its process is because you need to be comfortable and informed before litigating a consumer law case.

"Life Is A Challenge, Meet It! Life Is A Dream, Realize It!

Life Is A Game, Play It! Life Is Love, Enjoy It!"

Sathya Sai Baba

CHAPTER FIVE

How To Beat A Collection Agency In Court

There have been a lot of things that have changed in the debt collection business over the last several years. Many people are experiencing roadblocks as they try to remove collection accounts from their credit. For example, many consumers are the victims of debt parking and don't even know it. Just what is debt parking? Debt parking is when collection agencies put accounts on your credit file without notifying you that you even owe them any money. The problem with this practice is that by law, collection agencies must communicate with you first, if you in fact owe them money. When they do not communicate with the consumer first, this is a violation of the FTC Act, the Fair Debt Collections Practice Act and the Fair Credit

Reporting Act. This is also why I tell you, if a collection agency contacts you, always respond and tell them the debt does not belong to you.

There are also other ways to fight collection agencies other than through the mail. What is that way? Court! I am going to teach you how to put pressure on the collection agency to make them back up and run the other way. I am going to provide you with two different templates. First let me explain to you how to use written discovery against the collection agency. What is Discovery? It is the ability for each party in a lawsuit to obtain any documentation or any information related to the case.

Always remember that the same way the collection agency can request information from you, you can request information from them as well. You are able to do this because there are rules to discover case law and statutes that require that you provide any documentation pertaining to a lawsuit before you even go to court.

When you make a written discovery to a collection agency there are going to be three things that you ask for within the discovery. They should be as follow:

*Request for Admission (these are real specific questions, and you can only admit or deny)

*Request for Production

*Interrogatories (these are just written questions where you can request information from the creditor, and they can request information from you)

There is also another form of discovery that is called "Depositions" where you take oral testimony in front of a court reporter, but I do not think that type of Discovery is important for the simple fact I do not think that you will ever get that far, but I will advise you that in every state there are Rule 33-Interrogatories, Rule 34-Request for Production and Rule 36- Request for Admission. And most of these rules are based off of Federal Rules of Civil Procedures and they are the Rules that I just mentioned Rule 33, Rule 34 and Rule 36 and you actually can look these rules up online. If you want to go online and look these rules up so that you can be sure that they in fact match up with the rules in your state, you can find the Rules of Civil Procedure in two places. The first one you can find on Google Scholar http://scholar.google.com and the second one is Legal Information Institute http://law.cornell.edu.

Both of these websites are free. Remember all you have to type is "request for production" or "request for admissions."

John and Jane Doe
123 West Street
Anywhere, TN 38115
Defendant *Pro Se*

ANYWHERE SUPERIOR COURT

STATE OF TENNESSEE

Midland Funding, LLC, Plaintiff, vs. John and Jane Doe, Defendants	Case No. CV2021-000001 **MOTION TO DISMISS AND COMPEL PRIVATE ARBITRATION**

Defendants John and Jane Doe do hereby submit their Motion to Dismiss and Compel Private Arbitration as follows:

Plaintiff Midland Funding, LLC ("Midland Funding") filed its lawsuit against John and Jane Doe alleging that the original creditor was Credit One Bank. Credit One Bank Credit Card Agreements are provided on the website for the Consumer Financial Protection Bureau and contain the applicable terms for Credit One Bank credit card accounts.

The applicable agreement to this case expressly provides that the parties have waived their right to a trial and instead agree to submit any and all disputes, including due to a default, to private arbitration under the American Arbitration Association ("AAA"). *See* Credit Card Agreement, pp. 6-7, a true and accurate copy is attached as Exhibit A.

The Credit Card Agreement specifically states:

> **"This agreement to arbitrate provides that you or we can require controversies or disputes between us to be resolved by BINDING ARBITRATION.** *Id.* at p. 6.

The Card Agreement between Credit One Bank and John and Jane Doe permits either party to elect to participate in private arbitration. If the language of an arbitration agreement is clear, courts should afford it its plain and ordinary meaning and apply it as written.

Here, in this case, the arbitration clause is clear and there can be no dispute that this matter falls within the plain meaning of the agreement. John and Jane Doe hereby elect to submit this matter to private arbitration and invoke this clause in the Credit Card Agreement. Based upon this it is respectfully requested that this case be dismissed.

DATED this ______ day of May 2024.

____________________________ __________________________

John Doe Jane Doe

COPIES of the foregoing sent via U.S. mail on _____ day of May 2024 to:

Attorney

123 Law Firm Street

Anywhere, TN 38115

Attorney for the Plaintiff

By:____________________

"Life Is Like A Game Of Chess, Always

Think Before You Make A Move"

UnKnown

CHAPTER SIX

Should You Use Discovery?

The reason why you wanna ask yourself do you wanna use written discovery or not is because most people use this process incorrectly. Discovery is powerful because you have the courts at your disposal, because you have the power of the subpoena, and you can request documents through the civil process via written discovery.

Let's look at some reasons why you do not need to conduct written discovery. Always remember that the creditor/plaintiff must prove all the elements of their case. If they do not prove the elements of the case, they will not get a judgement. You do not have to disprove anything pertaining to the case. This is the reason you should provide them with as little information as you can, because the less information that they have, chances are they cannot prove their case. This is the reason why sometimes you may not want to make a case for written discovery because they may not have anything anyway.

Now on the other hand, one reason why you would conduct discovery is not to get documentation, but to force the creditor into making a choice whether they are going to disclose documents that you are requesting or dismiss the case. What are those documents you ask? Well, I'm going to show you the exact document that you want to request. Now keep in mind they are suing you and remember when I told you that written discovery works both ways and you have the power of the court, subpoenas, and admissions on your side. And this is when it will work in your favor.

The important thing to remember is to do this process correctly and not ask for too much information from the collection agency or creditor. You do not want to be a detriment to your own case and the collection agency go and get information that they didn't have at first. Remember the least amount of information they have the better. Remember the documents that you request should fall into two categories and those are documents they do not have and documents they do not want to turn over. And between the two categories, you want to request documents they do not have, because they do not want to be sent to the public.

The topics that they do not want you to have are called Forward Flow Agreements or sometimes called Purchase and Sale Agreement. The first thing that you need to do is get the complaint or the summons that they served you with, to see if there are any documents attached to that or you can look at the initial disclosures. Sometimes there won't be any documentation attached to it, but most of the time they do. If there is no documentation attached to the initial paperwork, just wait a few days because they have to be turned over at some point. Now what you want to be looking for in the complaint is the Bill of Assignment or Bill of Sale.

The reason why you want to look for these two documents is because within these documents is what's called a Master Purchase and Sale Agreement.

Now they will try to tell you that the Bill of Assignment or Bill of Sale is the full contract. It's Not! The Master Purchase and Sale Agreement is the full agreement, and this is the agreement that you want to request along with Exhibit 1. Now Exhibit 1 is going to look like a sentence so do not be fooled.

Just remember that what you want to be looking for when you receive documents from the collection agency is a Receivable Purchase Agreement, Purchase Agreement, Purchase and Sale Agreement or Forward Flow Agreement. These are the documents that you want because all they are trying to do is show a chain of command. I have provided the template that you need to request these documents from the collection agency below. Please remember to keep it simple and insert your information in the correct spaces.

Now once you request the documentation do not be surprised if they do not respond right away. You also, what to check and see how long they have to respond. Eventually they will respond with a letter of objection stating that what you are asking for is not relevant to the case. Well, that is not true because the Master Bill of Sale is supposed to give them the right to sue you. They did not loan you money and you did not agree to pay them any money. So, they have to show the court how they have standing or a right to sue you.

When they send you an objection letter, you then need to compel the court to make them produce the documents. So now that you have to get the court involved, I have provided you with the template to do this. You just need to customize it a little bit explaining what's going on. All you have to do is explain what you want and attach their response to you within your request. You want to make copies of everything you send out. If you need to go back to google scholar or legal information institute to get specific statues or rules that apply to your state, then do that as well.

Tell the court that you are entitled to the documentation that you are requesting. Most courts will set the matter for oral argument and have the plaintiff come in and say why they should have to turn over these documents, but a lot of courts will just say you must turn these documents over. Because these documents are relevant. They cannot come and state that there is proprietary information. For example, "how much they paid for the debt. You can even be flexible and tell the court that they can redact the price out, but you want the Master Purchase and Sale Agreement.

You want the Master Purchase and Sale Agreement because it is the document they claim gives them the right to sue you, it has all the disclaimers, warranties and everything else. The court will then issue an Order Compelling them to turn it over.

Once the court does this, they will then come to you with some low-ball settlement offer or they may just dismiss. Nine times out of ten they will just dismiss. When they say they will dismiss, you need to keep in mind that in most states they just cannot walk away. You have to agree to it. So, if they come with this saying they will dismiss, you need to make sure the case is dismissed with prejudice. Dismiss with Prejudice means they cannot file it again and they must give you a release from the debt. Either way you need to get something stating that they cannot collect on the balance moving forward and the case is dismissed with prejudice.

The thing that you need to remember is that they do not want this information out to the public because a lot of the disclaimers and warranties often are in these documents. The original creditor tells them that they cannot guarantee the correct dollar amount and the debt maybe outside the statute of limitations. They will also inform them that the debt could have been discharged in bankruptcy. But at the end of the day, the courts will compel them to turn over the documents you need.

Your Name
Your Address
Your City, State, Zip Code

YOUR COURT NAME

Creditor/Debt Buyer Name, Plaintiff, v. Your Name, Defendants.	Case No. **DEFENDANTS' MOTION TO COMPEL**

Defendants request the Court enter an order compelling Plaintiff to comply to Defendants' Request for Production of documents under Rule 34.

I. Statement of Facts (adjust to the facts of your case)

This action arises from Plaintiff's claim to be the owner in interest to a debt for which Defendants are liable. Plaintiff purports to have purchased the Defendant's debt after the debt was transferred: (1) from the original creditor, Citibank, N.A. to Distressed Asset Portfolio III, LLC; (2) from Distressed Asset Portfolio III, LLC to Distressed Asset Portfolio IV, LLC; and (3) from Distressed Asset Portfolio IV, LLC to Plaintiff.

On or around [insert date you send the Request for Production], Defendants sent a copy of Defendant's Request for Production to Plaintiff, attached hereto as *Exhibit A*. In this Request, Defendants sought documents relating both substantively to the accounts terms and conditions to the transfers. Specifically, in this Request, Defendants sought the following:

(1) "Copy of the 'Master Purchase and Sale Agreement dated August 09, 2017 and Addendum No. 5 dated March 29, 2018' referenced in the Bill of Sale and Assignment between Citibank, N.A. and Distressed Asset Portfolio III, LLC." (Defendants attached a copy of the Bill of Sale and Assignment to their Request for Production showing a reference to the documents requested).

(2) "Copy, in its completeness and entirety, of 'Exhibit 1' referenced in the Bill of Sale and Assignment between Citibank, N.A. and Distressed Asset Portfolio III, LLC." (Defendants attached an extract from the requested Exhibit 1 in their Request for Production for reference).

On or around [insert date plaintiff responded], Plaintiff responded to Defendants' Request for Production with a general objection for each of the two (2) requests. These objections were all the same, and verbatim, were:

> "The request is overly broad, unduly burdensome, irrelevant, confidential, proprietary and not reasonably calculated to lead to the discovery of admissible evidence. Further, the request is not limited in time or scope."

A copy of Plaintiff's response is attached hereto as *"Exhibit B."*

II. <u>Legal Argument (adjust as needed)</u>

A. <u>Defendants are entitled to an order compelling Plaintiff to comply with Rule 34.</u>

Each of the Defendants' requests is relevant to the subject of the case at hand. The purpose of each request made is to require Plaintiff to establish, through documentation, a transparent chain of title for the Defendants' debt. As such a chain of title is necessary for Plaintiff to prevail in this matter, the requested documentation is not irrelevant.

Defendant's requests are intended to seek confirmation that Defendants' debt was transferred between the companies indicated above. Defendants' have no need or desire for the account information for the other debts not belonging to Defendants transferred between these companies. As such, Plaintiff may redact the documents to maintain the confidentiality of other third parties, but they should be required to disclose the evidence in their original form rather than in "extracts" that were created at a different time and place than the original documents. As such, the requested records do not require confidential information to be disclosed.

WHEREFORE, Defendants respectfully request the following:

1. Enter an Order to Compel Plaintiff to disclose the documents requested in Defendants' Request for Production;
2. All other relief the Court may deem proper and just.

DATED this ____day of July 2021.

____

Your Name

COPY of the following sent this ___day of July 2024

via U.S. Mail and electronically to:

Creditor Attorney Name

Creditor Attorney Address

Creditor Attorney City, State, Zip

Attorney for Plaintiff

By: ____

"Life Is A Game, Play It....Life Is Too Precious, Do Not Destroy It"

Mother Teresa

CHAPTER SEVEN

Filing A Motion To Strike Affidavit Of Debt

If you are in the middle of a lawsuit, hopefully you have already read how to answer a summons and complaint and how a lawsuit works. Having digested all of that information, you are now ready to move on to the next phase of your lawsuit, filing a Motion to Strike because part of what you received along with your Summons and Complaint is an Affidavit of Debt from the Plaintiff.

An affidavit is a sworn statement inwriting, so therefore, an affidavit of debt is a sworn statement from an employee of the Plaintiff (i.e., collection agency) stating they are intimately familiar and/or aware of the methods of record keeping at the original creditor concerning the debt in question, and they can certify the information in the complaint is true. They also usually state that they have examined the sale or assignment records that establish the relationship between the original creditor selling/assigning to the collection agency or junk debt buyer.

Note: These affidavits are sometimes notarized, but their validity is unchanged whether or not this is the case.

If you, the Defendant, do not object to this affidavit, the court will assume the debt is valid and the debt collector will have the right to sue you, and the suit is proper. You will lose if this happens. Fortunately, most of the time these affidavits are fraudulent or contain false evidence, but you must file a motion to strike so that this evidence can get thrown out of court.

Here is an example of an affidavit of debt:

Plaintiff's Affidavit of Indebtedness and Ownership of Account

I am an authorized representative for ACME Collection Agency (hereafter the "Plaintiff") and hereby certify as follows:

1. I have personal knowledge regarding Plaintiff's creation and maintenance of its normal business records including computer records of accounts receivables. This information was regularly and contemporaneously maintained during the course of the Plaintiff's business. I am authorized to execute this affidavit on behalf of Plaintiff

and the information below is true and correct to the best of my knowledge, information and belief based on business records maintained with respect to the account.

2. The records provided to Plaintiff have been represented to include information provided by the original creditor. Such information includes the debtor's name, social security number, account balance, and identity of the original creditor and account number.

3. Based on the business records maintained on account XXXXXXX3452 (hereafter "account"), which are a compilation of the information provided upon acquisition and information obtained since acquisition, the

account is the result of the extension of credit to "name" by original creditor, on or about (date of the origination). Said business records further indicate the account was then owned by ACME Huge Bank. Acme Huge Bank later sold and/or assigned portfolio 8044 to Plaintiff's assignor which included the defendant's account on (date of assignment). Thereafter, all ownership rights were assigned to, transferred to, and became vested in Plaintiff, including the right to collect the purchased balance owing $1,487.65 plus any additional accrued interest.

4. To the best of my knowledge and belief, the Defendant is not a minor or mentally incompetent.

5. Based on business records maintained in regard to the account, the above stated amounts are justly and duly owed by the Defendant to the Plaintiff and that all just and lawful offsets, payments, and credits to the account have been allowed. Demand for payment was made more than 30 days ago.

Signed,

Clueless Employee

ACME Collection Agency

Sound like bullshit? Don't worry, I'll show you how this affidavit is nonsense and complete hearsay.

Combat False Affidavits Based On Hearsay Rules

Attack the authority of the person writing the affidavit:

1. Subpoena the Affiant (person writing the affidavit) to appear in court for testimony. Usually this person will be "unavailable."
2. File a subpoena for the employment record and resume of the Affiant. There may be some fighting by the Plaintiff's attorney but since they are claiming to be knowledgeable, this is not an unreasonable request.
3. Does the employee look like he or she has knowledge of record keeping? If this person has only been employed to contact debtors on the telephone, obviously there is no experience.

4. If the Affiant's experience looks questionable, pose the question as to how he/she can know the original creditor's methods of keeping records.
5. What if the Affiant is employed by the original issuer of the credit card? Even if he/she is an employee of the original creditor, does he/ she have proper experience to be a record keeper?
6. Cite the case law given here showing that affidavits are known to be false and misleading.
7. Stated in your motion filed with the court that "the Affiant's employment resume shows he/she cannot have knowledge of the original creditor's bookkeeping practices, and the fact that she/he is not available to

testify in court and may not even exist along with the past used of falsified affidavits in other states by this JBD points to this affidavit of being highly suspect and should be stricken."

8. Does the Affiant have the necessary background to be a record keeper? If so, is there a claim they are familiar with the original creditor's record keeping? What is the proof for their statements?
9. Cite cases where affidavits are purported to be made on personal knowledge, but in fact are based on reading a computer screen.
10. File your motion to strike the affidavit of debt with the court.
11. At this point, the affidavit should be stricken, and hopefully the case will be dismissed.

PLEASE DO NOT JUST CUT AND PASTE as every motion is different. One size does not fit all. If you merely cut and paste, you will lose the case. In addition, you need to review and understand your state/county Rules of Civil Procedures when filing your motion. Improper filing of your motion will cause it to be denied.

SAMPLE MOTION TO STRIKE PLAINTIFF'S OF DEBT

IN THE JUSTICE COURT OF (City Name)

County Name, STATE OF

Case Number: XXXX564

Collection Agency,

Plaintiff

vs

John Q. Smith

Defendant

MOTION TO STRIKE AFFIDAVIT OF DEBT IN SUPPORT OF PLAINTIFF'S CLAIMS

Comes now, Defendant and respectfully states the following:

1. Plaintiff has submitted into evidence an affidavit claiming that the affiant has personal knowledge of business records related to the aforementioned debt. AFFIDAVIT OF DEBT IN SUPPORT OF PLAINTIFF'S CLAIMS (hereinafter referred to as EXHIBIT A").
2. The affiant writing the AFFIDAVIT OF DEBT (Exhibit A) does not explain how the business records came into his/her possession, only that to the best of his/her

belief they “represent” the actual records from the original creditor, Gigantic Credit Card Company.

3. Affiant of AFFIDAVIT OF DEBT does not claim to have personal knowledge of how business records were kept at the original creditor.
4. Affiant of AFFIDAVIT OF DEBT does not claim to have personal knowledge of the sale or assignment of the debt from the original creditor to ACME Collection Agency.

WHEREFORE, the Defendant prays this Honorable Court that Plaintiff’s “Exhibit A” be sticken from evidence in the above action.

I state under penalty of perjury that the foregoing is true and correct.

Defendant Name.

By:_______________________________ Date:______

Defendant Name, Defendant

Address

Phone

I CERTIFY that I mailed/delivered a copy of this MOTION to: ACME Collection Attorney

Address

Plaintiff's attorney at the above address or Defendant's attorney

By:_____________________________ Date:__________

Defendant Name, Defendant

Please Note: I AM NOT AN ATTORNEY. If you are being sued, its always a good idea to hire an attorney or get some legal assistance. If you cannot afford an attorney, a lot of people have handled their cases pro per or without a lawyer.

"Life Is Like A Game, There Could Be Many Players.

If You Don't Play With Them, They'll Play With You"

Adolf Hitler

CHAPTER EIGHT

DISPUTE LETTERS

LETTER TO REMOVE INACCURATE CREDIT INFORMATION

Name

Address

DOB

SSN

Credit Bureau

Date

Re: Letter to Remove Inaccurate Credit Information

To Whom It May Concern:

I received a copy of my credit report with the intention of purchasing a vehicle. In the process I noticed a few accounts that I wanted a little more information on. I am not saying they are reporting right or wrong. I am just saying that I am not positive if they are. In the process of researching I found something called Fair Credit Reporting Act where it said by law, I had rights to challenge anything I am not sure is reporting a 100% accurate. Some of the creditors reporting things on my credit profile, I have never heard of which made me write you all.

1. Example

Account Number: 534339172

Please investigate if every piece of information is correct. If not, please remove it from my credit report.

After researching consumer laws, I found 15 U.S.C. Sec. 1681i(a)? I heard that if you can't provide proof, these accounts must be deleted. Well, I want these accounts deleted if they are not 100 percent right and correct. So, could you please check on these and get back with me. Please investigate the following accounts and remove them if anything is missing or not correct on them.

Also, can I receive an updated copy of my credit report. Also, please let me know who had access to my file as well. I want the investigation outcome to be sent to the address I put on the from area.

Thank you for your time and help in this matter.

LETTER TO REMOVE STUDENT LOAN ACCOUNTS

Date

Name

Address

Date of Birth

SSN

TransUnion LLC Consumer Dispute Center

PO Box 2000

Chester, PA 19016

In my previous dispute letter, I provided enough information for you to carry out an investigation on these accounts. For each account listed, I detailed the creditor name, account number and exact reason for dispute. I am aware that these are the 3 elements that are required for you to perform an investigation. I would like to know why you have sent me a stall letter instead of removing or correcting these per my requests. In case my intent was not clear: Please perform an investigation of the items I have listed below. I have detailed the dispute reasons with the facts taken directly from my credit report with your organization. In the event that you return with a response that these are still accurate, I will need you to furnish all documentation that was used during this investigation. These are my disputed accounts:

1. US DEPT ED

   Account Number: 4218

   How is it that two credit bureaus are reporting closed status and the other open? This is inaccurate, please have this removed from my credit report

2. US DEPT ED

   Account Number: XXX

   I didn't provide permission for this account to be reporting to my credit report. Please remove or I will seek legal action

3. US DEPT ED

   Account Number: XXX

   This account was not verified by the other credit bureaus so how did you verify this account is mine? I demand this account be removed.

4. DPT ED/NAVI

   Account Number: 986741E0022010

   This account was not verified to be mine. Please remove this account from my profile immediately

5. DPT ED/NAVI

   Account Number: 986741E0032010

   This account was not verified to be mine. Please remove this account from my profile immediately

6. DPT ED/NAVI

   Account Number: 986741E0012008

I didn't give permission for this account to be reporting to my credit report. please have this account removed or I will seek legal action

7. HWARFIELD

   Account Number: 63043

   How is it that one bureau is reporting this to my credit profile as open and the other closed? Please have this account removed from my credit profile immediately. Also, can I receive an updated copy of my credit report? Also, please let me know who had access to my file as well. I want the investigation outcome to be sent to the address I put on the from area. Thank you for your time and help in this matter.

LETTER TO DISPUTE IDENTITY THEFT

Date

Name

Address

Date of Birth

CB Address

This letter is to inform you and your company that I'm a victim of **IDENTITY THEFT**! The accounts that are listed below do not belong to me. This is my 3rd time contacting your company to resolve this issue and you still report these fraudulent items on my credit report. Conspiracy is defined by black laws dictionary as "A combination or confederacy between two or more persons formed for the purpose of committing, by their joint efforts, some unlawful or criminal act, or some act which is innocent in itself, but becomes unlawful when done by the concerted action of the conspirators, or for the purpose of using criminal or unlawful means to the commission of an act not in itself». After contacting you and the listed creditors below, Ive received no verification these accounts are mine. Which has led me to believe your company and the listed names below are conspiring to defame my character. Your actions of subterfuge have violated my rights under the **FAIR CREDIT REPORTING ACT. Under the FCRA of 1970 Section 609(e)** I request that all the information listed on my report to be deleted from my consumer credit file

I demand the following accounts be verified or removed immediately.

1. Account Name

Account Number:

Thank You,

INTENT TO SUE LETTER

Date

Name

Address

Date of Birth:

CB Address

I am sure you are aware that it is against the law to threaten suit without any intention of doing so. Therefore, be advised that I am extremely serious about filing a suit against your company. I have sent numerous letters requesting you to investigate and remove all inaccurate information that is being reported on my personal credit profile, yet you continue to fail to do so. It is my understanding of the law that you MUST honor each and every request to investigate incorrect information and you seem to have ignored all of my previous requests. That is a crystal-clear violation of the Fair Credit Reporting Act which provides a cause of action for an individual consumer as well as penalties and liabilities for both consumer reporting agencies and furnishers of information for non-compliance as violation of its provisions. As I stated before, this is my final request for you to do as you are governed by the FCRA. If this final request does not prompt you to conduct a proper investigation of the accounts in question, I will be forced to file a suit against your company in the county in which I live. That way, you can travel here in order to defend yourselves. I take my credit very serious, and your lack of professionalism and assistance disgusts me. I am well aware of my rights under the FCRA and intend to pursue them to the maximum. I am anticipating your immediate response.

This is the last time I will demand the following accounts be verified or removed immediately.

1. Account Name

Account Number:

Thank You,

LETTER TO REQUEST AN INVESTIGATION FOR COLLECTION/LATE ACCOUNT

(First, Last, M.I.) (Street)

(City, State, Zip)

(Credit Bureau) (Address)

(Bureau City, State, ZIP) (Date)

Investigation Request Letter

Date of Birth: Jan 1, 1982

SS#:XXX-XX-1234 (Enter Only Last 4 of SSN)

To Whom It May Concern:

I received a copy of my credit report with the intention of trying to improve my credit and take care of my responsibilities and noticed a few accounts that I wanted a little more explanation on. I am not saying they are reporting right or wrong. I am just saying that I am not 100 percent sure if they are. I also read something called the Fair Credit Reporting Act where it said by law, I had rights to challenge anything I am not sure is accurate. Some of the people reporting things on me, I have never heard of which made me write you all.

Are you familiar with something called 15 U.S.C. Sec. 1681i(a)? I heard that if you can't provide proof, these accounts must be deleted. Well, I want these accounts deleted if they are not 100 percent right and correct. So, could you please check on these and get back with me? I saw on a Credit Site and Board where this lawyer said you have 30 days to complete this investigation. Please investigate the following accounts and remove them if anything is missing or not correct on them.

Type of Account:

Public Record: Case Number:

Action Requested: Please provide proof that its reporting correctly from the Court House and not a third party and delete if anything is incorrect.

Collection Account:

Account Number:

Please investigate if every piece of information is correct. If not, please remove it from my credit report.

Paid Account/Late Payments:

Account Number:

Please investigate if every piece of information is correct in the reported late payment history. If the late payments are not reporting 100 percent accurate, please remove them from this account and update the account as "paid as agreed."

I also read where I can get the updated report after you investigate this from the Free Lawyer guy. Could you please send it to me? Also, please let me know who had access to my file as well. I want the investigation outcome to be sent to the address I put on the from area.

Thank you for your time and help in this matter. Sincerely,

LETTER TO REQUEST REINVESTIGATION

John Doe Sr

123 Easy Street

Atlanta, Georgia 30301

Equifax Information Services LLC

P.O. Box 740256

Atlanta, GA 30348

Attn.: Consumer Relations

Department

To Whom It May Concern,

I want to start by saying thank you for looking at the items I sent in for investigation. Upon investigating the accounts, I investigated directly from the source furnishing the data to you to ensure that everything matches up as well. Upon looking at the history between all 3 credit bureaus, I wanted to point out the inconsistencies in the reporting in the following accounts.

Account Name: Credit One

Account Number: XXXXX6778

Errors Found(examples): High Credit shows $xx, but no months are showing in the report of that balance on the reports on TU, but not EQ. The terms differ in months on TU, EX, and EQ which is not possible on accurate accounts. The open date on each account has different months on it, which is no possible way the accounts were opened on 3 different days.

Action: Please Delete Immediately

Account Name: Medical Collections USA

Account Number: XXXXX6778

Errors Found(examples):

The terms in the collection stated 6 months. I never signed a term agreement for any medical bill in which the terms cannot be 6 months on a dead collections account. The date of this collection account is wrong as it does not state the original date the account went into collections.

Action: Please Delete Immediately

I understand the process of the investigation is to reach every.

Individual company to verify the accuracy of the information. In accordance with FCRA, Section 611 A through D, you are supposed to let me know who you verified with.

In my original investigation request sent (date) I asked you to delete anything that is not 100 percent accurate. This is not the time to update since you had time to update after the first letter. Now that I have pointed out the mistakes, updating the terms is an admission of guilt and direct violation of my rights of a fair investigation. You stated it was verified. How is it possible that TransUnion, Equifax, and Experian all verified the accounts above as accurate, but they all have inconsistencies in the reporting? In fact, there is no possible way a full investigation could have been done in accordance with Section 611 due to the inconsistencies coming after my original request for investigation. At this point, I demand you delete these accounts immediately, or I have no choice but to seek counsel to point out the rights that have been violated under the FCRA. Please forward me an updated credit report after you have completed your deletions and corrections. Sincerely your

CLAIM OF FRAUDLENT ACCOUNT- COLLECTION AGENCY

Your Name

Address

City/State/Zip

Phone Number

Email address if appropriate

RE: Credit Card or Bank Acct #________

Check #_______

Date:

Dear Sirs:

This letter is provided as legal notice to inform you that on or about ______(date), the following occurred:

_____ Checks numbered xxx to xxx for ___ (bank name, acct #xxx) were stolen. Be advised that this account was closed on ____ (date) by the bank upon my request.

_____ Checks numbered xxx, xxx, xxx have been fraudulently created by another person using my name and address as the account holder.

_____ A credit card was opened without my authorization or knowledge, using my name, social security number and other personal data. Card #______________

_____ Credit card # xxx was stolen and then used by the thief. Be advised that this. account was closed on ___ (date) when I directly called the credit card company and told them of the theft.

_____ Other (explain) ____

These checks/credit cards are now or were being fraudulently used to obtain goods and services from merchants. You are officially being told that this is a case of identity theft or financial fraud and that an investigation is required at this time.

Please be advised that appropriate agencies and companies have been notified. You are free to contact any of these agencies to verify this information. If available, a copy of the police report will be attached to this letter.

Name of police department fraud was reported to: ___________________________

Contact person and phone number ______________________________

Bank: ______________________________

Contact person and phone number ______________________________

Credit Card company ______________________________

Contact person and phone number ______________________________

I have also notified the three major credit reporting agencies, Equifax, Experian and TransUnion, placed a fraud alert on my account and notified them of possible fraudulent activity. Where appropriate, I have also notified the following check verification companies: ______________________________

Please advise your client or the assignor of this criminal activity and notify them not to reassign this account to another agency. So far, these criminals have stolen approximately $______ in checks or credit charges in my name. We suspect there will be more until they are caught.

Now that you have been notified in writing about the fraud-- Be advised that reporting these items to the credit bureaus as collection items or continuing to pursue these debts from me prior to an investigation would be considered a violation of the state and federal level Fair Debt Collection Practices Act and the Fair Credit Reporting Act.

I hereby request photocopies of any applications, application information or transaction information you may have on this account. (Required by law-FACTA effective June 2, 2004) It will be turned over to law enforcement so that this criminal might be brought to justice.

This has been a very frustrating experience for me. I have always maintained an impeccable credit history. I appreciate your circumstances and hope you can appreciate mine. It is my hope that the law enforcement agencies can apprehend these criminal(s) and put them in jail. Until that time, I will have to continue to deal with this unpleasant situation. Regrettably so will the merchants who unknowingly accept these checks/credit cards.

I declare under penalty of perjury that this declaration is true and correct to the best of my knowledge. **Knowingly submitting false information on this affidavit could subject me to criminal prosecution for perjury.**

Sincerely,

______________________________ ______________

Name Date

Non-relative witness to signature: (Print Name) ______________________________

Witness signature______________________________ Date______________

Corey P Smith

Witness phone number____________________

AFFIDAVIT OF IDENTITY AND STATEMENT FACTS

STATE OF YOUR STATE

COUNTY OF DALLAS

I, the affiant herein, being first duly sworn upon oath does hereby state:

1. That my legal name is [full name].
2. That my U.S. Government Number (SSN or ITIN) is [social]
3. That my current Physical Address Is (will not accept a PO Box)

[primary address _street] [primary _address city] [primary address state) [primary address postal code]

4. That my date of birth is [date of birth]
5. That I did present to my Notary Public, as proof of my identity, a valid state/U. S Government issued Photo ID

Type [] Driver's License [ ] Identification [ ] Card Other (please describe)

Issued in the state of: ______________________________ (required id Driver's License or ID Card selected)

Number: ______________________________

6. That the purpose of this Affidavit is to establish and verify that the Affiant is the same as the individual whose records are being kept by TransUnion, Equifax (CSC Credit Services Inc.), Experian, and Innovis.
7. That the Affiant understands that falsification to any degree of this Affidavit is a felony criminal offense and will subject such Affiant to prosecution to the fullest extent of the law.

AFFIANT FURTHER STATES THE FACTS:

1. I should not be associated with [address]. It should not appear on my credit report.
2. I should not be associated with [phone]. It should not appear on my credit report.
3. I should not be associated with [social]. It should not appear on my credit report.
4. I should not be associated with [birthdate]. It should not appear on my credit report.

Signature of Affiant ____
Print Full Legal Name of Affiant ____________________________________
Current Telephone Number OF Affiant ______________________________

Notary Public:

Subscribed and sworn to (or affirmed) before me on this _________ day of _______________. 20_____ by ____[full name of affiant], provided to me on the basis of presentation of satisfactory evidence to be the person(s) who appeared before me.

____

Notary Signature

"Life Is A Game, You Can Be A Player Or A Toy"

UnKnown

CHAPTER NINE

Always Be Three Moves Ahead

I have always tried to live my life to the fullest and anything that I became interested in, I became obsessed with it. You see, life really is like a game. Remember at the beginning of the book when I told you that my dad taught me two games in life. I gave you my opinion about how life is like a monopoly game and now I will explain how knowing how to play chess will help you navigate life as well.

Life is nothing more than competition. For example, schools dumb you down to believe that you have to follow a certain blueprint in order to succeed in life. Success is defined more by a person's status rather than happiness, even though the older you get in life the more you figure out that happiness and health are the most important pieces that you give have in this game of life. Your financial vibration is your credit score, physical health is your blood pressure, and education is measured based on your grades and test scores.

When you start to see that life is nothing more than a spiritual game, things will change. So, what does chess have to do with life, well when you begin to see the comparisons, your mind becomes open to new ways of living. Most of our choices and actions appear unimportant to our futures so we act quickly. We fail to see the relationship between each decision and often it is only a matter of time before we end up losing. Author Allan Rufus said, "Life is like a game of chess. To win you have to make a move. Knowing which move to make comes with insight and knowledge, and by learning the lessons that are gained along the way. We become each and every piece within the game called life."

The most important sentence is this: "Knowing which move to make comes with insight and knowledge, and by learning the lessons that are gained along the way." Insight and knowledge are the connections which exist unseen between every sing decision you make and every consequence you create. The same logic applies when playing chess. Every single piece moved matters and life is no different. The game of life demands we play many games often at the same time and knowing what prize the winner gets for winning is not always clear. Life is a game that each one of us must play.

www.ingramcontent.com/pod-product-compliance
Lightning Source LLC
LaVergne TN
LVHW022304200926
848481LV00004B/1205
* 9 7 9 8 2 9 5 6 2 3 2 4 0 *